A Black Hero

By. Gilbert Vaughn

Published by Vision 2 Impact 2026

www.visions2impact.com

www.visions2impact.com

TABLE OF CONTENTS

Prologue

An Eye Sees Everything But Itself

An eye sees everything but itself. That is something I learned a long time ago. A man can spend his whole life looking out at the world, watching what happens around him, and still not fully understand his own story. You see other people's victories, their mistakes, their tragedies, and their blessings. But sometimes it takes many years before you step back and really look at your own life. Now at seventy-eight years old, I suppose it is time I try.

Time changes, but people do not. The world looks different now than it did when I was a boy, but human nature has stayed mostly the same. It still takes all kinds of people to make up this world. If you live long enough, you will see kindness and cruelty, courage and fear, wisdom and foolishness. Sometimes you see all of it in the same day. Life has a way of teaching lessons whether you are ready for them or not. Some lessons come through joy. Others come through loss. But every experience leaves something behind. The older you get, the more you realize that life is really a collection of moments. Some big, some small. Some you wish you could forget, and others you wish you could relive one more time.

One thing I have learned after all these years is not to take life too seriously. Nobody gets out alive anyway. So, you might as well enjoy the ride while you are here. Laugh when you can. Learn when you must. And never forget that every day you wake up is another opportunity to do something good with the time you have been given. This is my story. I was not famous. I was not rich. But I lived a life full of experiences that shaped who I became. I saw history change right in front of my eyes. I saw the best and worst of humanity through my work in public service. I traveled to places I never imagined I would see when I was a boy growing up in St. Louis. And along the way, I learned a few things worth passing on.

CHAPTER ONE
Blue and White Beginnings

I was born May 23, 1947, to A.C. and Effie Vaughn at Homer G. Phillips Hospital in St. Louis, Missouri. At that time Homer G. Phillips was one of the largest hospitals serving the Black community in the country. Thousands of babies in St. Louis came into the world there. For many families, it was the only hospital that would treat them with dignity. My favorite colors for years were blue and white. I always believed that was because my baby blanket was blue and white. Funny how something as simple as a blanket can stay in your memory longer than some people do. I can still picture it in my mind after all these years. We lived at 3028 Thomas Street in St. Louis. That house does not exist anymore. Sometimes I drive by the area where it used to stand. There is nothing there now. Just empty space where memories once lived.

That is one of the strange things about time. Places that once meant everything to you can disappear without leaving a trace. But in my mind, that neighborhood still exists exactly the way it did when I was a boy. One of my earliest memories is watching my father build a small brick walkway from the curb to the sidewalk. I must have been about four years old. Now the truth is it probably was not anything special to most people. It certainly was not the eighth wonder of the world. But to a little boy watching his father work with his hands, it seemed important. I remember standing there watching him place each brick carefully into the ground, one by one. He took his time, making sure each one was lined up just right.

That moment stayed with me because it was one of the first times I saw what it meant to build something with patience. Years later I went back to see if that walkway was still there. I could not find it. That is life. The things we think will last forever sometimes disappear without warning. I had a sister named Brenda and a brother named Alfred. I was the youngest of the three. Being the baby of the family has its advantages when you are young. People look out for you. Your older siblings sometimes protect you from trouble. But when you grow older you begin to realize something else. Being the baby just means you will likely outlive more of the people you love. Both of them have passed away now.

When you reach a certain age, memories become a kind of family album in your mind. You remember things you did not even realize were important at the time. Next door to us lived a man who owned the prettiest chestnut horse you ever saw. Back in those days it was not unusual for people to keep horses in the city. Men known as rag collectors would travel through the alleys with horse drawn carts collecting various items. I never fully understood what they were collecting, but I remember hearing the sound of hooves hitting the pavement long before you actually saw the horse turn the corner. The neighborhood had its own rhythm back then. People burned their trash in metal barrels because there was no city trash pickup like we have today. Smoke drifting through the neighborhood was a normal sight.

You could walk down the alley and smell different things burning in different barrels. That was just part of everyday life. On Franklin Avenue, which they now call Martin Luther King Drive, there was a large brick circle that collected rainwater. The rag men would bring their horses there to drink. You could hear the horses before you saw them. The sound of hooves on pavement would echo through the street, and every kid in the neighborhood would look up to see what was coming. Another regular visitor to the neighborhood was the ice man.

Before refrigerators became common, people kept their food cold using iceboxes. The ice man would deliver large blocks of ice that families would place inside their iceboxes to keep food from spoiling. That was considered modern living at the time. I remember watching him carry those blocks of ice with big metal tongs. The ice would drip water down his arms as he walked from house to house. When refrigerators finally started showing up in homes, people thought we had entered the future. Things change faster than you expect.

I remember a neighbor named Mack Lucas who lived next door. He had been born sometime in the 1890s. As a young boy, I had never heard of anyone being born in the eighteen hundreds. It sounded almost impossible to me. But later in life I realized there were many people around who had lived through times we only read about in history books. My great uncle James Visor was another unforgettable figure in our family. When he was only five years old, he was kicked in the head by a mule. The injury affected him for the rest of his life. He was never quite the same afterward. But our family took care of him. Back then families did not send relatives away to institutions. Family handled family. Love meant responsibility. People looked after each other because that was simply what you did.

My uncle lived until he was fifty-six years old, and throughout that time different members of the family made sure he had a place to stay and people who cared for him. That is how things worked back then. Families carried each other. And in many ways, that is the kind of strength that shaped my life from the very beginning. I also remember my mother's twin sister, Lessie Avant, who lived at 4834 Northland in St. Louis. Back then, that was considered a beautiful neighborhood where what we called rich folks lived. You could see the difference as soon as you arrived. The homes were well kept, the streets were clean, and everything just felt a little more polished than what I was used to.

My aunt and uncle, Maurice Avant, lived a good life. To me as a young boy, it looked like they had everything. I remember visiting their home and just taking it all in. My uncle Maurice had a routine about him. Every morning, he would sit down, quiet and focused, reading the newspaper like a man who understood the importance of knowing what was going on in the world. One of the things that always stood out to me was the milkman. He came through the neighborhood with a horse drawn buggy, and what amazed me most was that the horse seemed to know the route better than the man driving it. That horse would stop at each house like clockwork, like it had done it a thousand times before.

My uncle Maurice also made sure I experienced life beyond just watching. He took me hunting, fishing, and to ball games. Those moments meant more than I understood at the time. Looking back now, I realize he was teaching me without saying much. Just by spending time, he was showing me what it looked like to be present, to provide, and to enjoy life. Growing up, you paid attention to the people around you. Not just what they said, but what they did. Where I'm from, everybody knew somebody who was trying to make something out of themselves. I remember knowing a young man from the neighborhood who went on to play for the Detroit Lions. I learned that you never really know what a person may become. Sometimes, greatness can be found in the most ordinary places if someone is willing to work hard, stay focused, and believe in themselves.

As a young boy growing up in St. Louis, we had a paperboy named Billy Sims. Billy Sims was the paper boy, and he lived across the street from me back in

1978 on the 5700 block of Terry. Every morning like clockwork, he'd be out there doing his route, his dog right by his side like they were a team. Rain, cold, or heat didn't matter, he showed up and handled his responsibility. I used to watch that, not realizing at the time how much it was teaching me. There was something about that routine that stuck with me. It wasn't just about delivering papers, it was about discipline, consistency, and doing what you said you were going to do. That image never left me. Until this day, I still read the paper every morning.

Back then, reading the paper wasn't just about headlines, it was about learning the world. It gave me perspective beyond my block, beyond what I saw every day. It showed me how people lived, what people were facing, and what was possible. It made me think bigger. Reading taught me how to slow down and pay attention. It helped me understand people, situations, and decisions in a different way. It sharpened how I saw life. While some people just glanced at the news, I studied it. I started connecting things, asking questions, and forming my own thoughts. He was simply the neighborhood kid delivering newspapers. Nobody could have imagined that the same young man riding through the neighborhood would one day become one of the greatest football players in America.

Billy Sims went on to attend the University of Oklahoma, win the prestigious Heisman Trophy, and play professionally in the NFL. His story serves as a reminder that greatness does not always announce itself early. Many times, it begins with humble beginnings, determination, and a dream. That is why we should never underestimate anyone, especially our young people. The child delivering newspapers today could become tomorrow's leader, teacher, doctor, athlete, firefighter, or hero. Every person has potential, and with faith, perseverance, and opportunity, amazing things can happen. You never know who is watching, who is learning, or who is quietly preparing for their moment. Greatness can come from anywhere. It showed me that people from where we stood could go further than what we saw on our block. It didn't feel like a dream or something far away. It felt real, because he was real. You could point to him and say, "He came from here." Those kinds of examples stick with you as a kid. They make you look at things a little differently. You start to realize that where you start doesn't have to be where you finish. At that age, you may not have all the words for it, but you understand one thing clearly, it's possible. And sometimes, that's all a young person needs to see.

Mongoose & Hurricane Production

—Presents—

All Star Professional Kick Boxing

CHAPTER TWO

The White Horse That Never Came

When I was about four years old, my mother would sometimes drop me off at a babysitter named Miss Frankie who lived upstairs next door. At that age I did not understand why she was leaving me there. In my young mind I thought I must have done something wrong. Children often believe everything that happens revolves around them. It took me a few years to realize that my mother was simply going to work and doing what she needed to do to take care of the family. Back then parents did not always explain everything to children. They just did what needed to be done.

While I stayed with Miss Frankie, I would often sit near the window waiting for my brother and sister to come home from school. They were older than me, and I looked up to them. One day my brother Alfred told me he rode a white horse. I believed him. I was too young to question it. Later my grandmother added to the story and told me that I would be getting a white horse of my own someday. From that day forward I watched for it. Every time the mailman walked down the street, I ran outside expecting him to deliver my horse. Day after day I waited. That horse never came. Even now, all these years later, I still laugh about that story. But it also taught me something important about people. You can fix your tongue to say anything.

Words can paint pictures in someone's mind whether they are true or not. Children believe what they are told. Sometimes adults do too. And sometimes life teaches you the difference between imagination and reality. But I will say this. For a while there, that white horse felt very real to me. And sometimes hope, even when it turns out to be wrong, is still a beautiful thing. Being one of the younger ones in the house, you learn your place early. Not because somebody sits you down and explains it, but because you're watching everything. You're paying attention to how things move, how decisions get made, and how the older ones carry themselves. You don't always get the first say. You don't always get the first chance. But what you do get is a front-row seat to how things work.

You learn how to listen more than you talk. You learn how to read the room. You pick up on what matters and what doesn't. And in a house with multiple personalities, you figure out quickly how to adjust, when to step forward, and when to step back. At the same time, being the younger one builds something in you. It gives you a quiet determination. You start wanting to prove yourself, not by talking about it, but by showing it. You watch what's already been done, and you think about how you're going to do your part in your own way.

There's also a different kind of bond that comes with siblings. It's not always said out loud, but it's there. You look out for each other. You learn from each other. Sometimes you compete, sometimes you disagree, but at the end of the day, that connection shapes how you deal with people for the rest of your life. Looking back, being the younger sibling didn't put me behind. If anything, it gave me time to observe, to learn, and to build my own approach before stepping into my own lane.

CHAPTER THREE

Indoor Toilets and Outhouses

People today would probably find it hard to believe that we once lived in a house without an indoor toilet. But that was reality for many families during those years. Before we had indoor plumbing, my sister Brenda had the responsibility each morning of taking what we called the pee pot outside. Yes, even in the city of St. Louis. We had an outhouse. When people hear that today they usually think of farms or country towns. But cities were not always as modern as people imagine. Plumbing did not reach every house at the same time. Life was different then. But it also shows just how quickly the world can change.

In just a few years we went from outhouses to indoor plumbing, from iceboxes to refrigerators, from horses in backyards to automobiles filling the streets. When indoor plumbing finally came to our house, it felt like we had stepped into the future. I remember adults talking about it like it was some kind of miracle. The same thing happened when televisions started appearing in homes. The first television I ever saw only had two channels. That was it. Everything was broadcast live. And at six o'clock in the evening the stations simply went off the air. The screen would turn blank and that was the end of television for the night. Imagine that today.

No twenty-four-hour channels. No streaming. No endless entertainment. When the television shut off, families talked to each other. Children played. Neighbors visited. Looking back now, I sometimes wonder if we did not lose something valuable when life became so busy and noisy. Back then the world forced people to slow down. And sometimes slowing down helps you notice what really matters.

Using the phone wasn't simple either. We had party lines, which meant the line was shared. Party lines were shared phone lines between multiple homes, so you were never the only one using it. You could pick up the receiver and hear a full conversation already in progress. If you needed to make a call, you had to speak up and ask if they could clear the line. Sometimes people were considerate and wrapped it up. Other times, they weren't in any hurry, especially if it wasn't urgent. You might just be told to wait. As a kid, that felt like the longest wait in the world.

There were also moments when folks would sit quiet on the line before saying anything, trying to figure out who was talking. Privacy wasn't guaranteed. You learned to be mindful of what you said and how you said it. It taught patience in a real way. You couldn’t rush the process, and you couldn’t control how other people handled it. You just had to adjust and make it work. At the time, it was normal. Everybody dealt with it the same way. But it’s one of those experiences that sticks with you, because it shows how people shared more than just space. They shared access, time, and sometimes even each other’s business whether they meant to or not.

CHAPTER FOUR

Grand Avenue and the Lines You Did Not Cross

Growing up in St. Louis during the nineteen fifties meant living in a world that was clearly divided by race. Grand Avenue served as an invisible line. If you crossed past Grand Avenue, you were entering the white part of town. Most Black families simply did not go there. It was not written on a sign, but everybody understood it. The Fox Theater downtown had a section where Black patrons were required to sit. It was upstairs in the balcony. They called it the "Negro Section." At the time that was simply the way things were. When you grow up in a world like that, you do not question it right away.

Children assume the world they see is normal. It takes time and experience before you begin to understand that things could be different. In 1955, when I was about eight years old, our family moved to 5706 Terry Avenue. At the time we were only the second Black family on that block. The only other Black resident was a woman named Miss Reggie. I did not fully understand racism yet, but I remember one moment very clearly. One day my mother sent my brother Alfred and me to a large grocery store to pick something up. When we walked inside, we saw more white people in one place than we had ever seen before. We froze.

Greater St. Louis Police Academy

Diploma

This diploma attests Gilbert Vaughn by his diligence and effort has satisfactorily completed the standard sixteen week course of basic instruction in police technique and procedure for the Police Service.

Awarded, this tenth day of May nineteen hundred and seventy three

Chairman, Board of Police Commissioners, St. Louis County — President, Board of Police Commissioners, City of St. Louis

Chairman, Board of Governors — Academy Director

Then we ran home. We burst through the door telling our mother what we had seen like we had just discovered something unbelievable. She listened calmly. Then she sent us right back to the store. "No fear," she said. That was one of the earliest lessons my mother taught us. The world might try to make you feel like you do not belong somewhere. But courage means walking through the door anyway. One of the qualities that shaped my childhood and ultimately influenced the path I would take in life was fearlessness. I was never the type to back down from a challenge or allow fear to dictate my decisions. That is not to say that I never experienced fear. Rather, I refused to let fear control me. Many of the activities I enjoyed required courage. Whether it was exploring the neighborhood, taking on new adventures, or stepping into unfamiliar situations, I developed a mindset early on that challenges were meant to be faced, not avoided. That willingness to move forward, even when the outcome was uncertain, became a defining characteristic of my life.

Having no fear does not mean recklessness. To me, it meant possessing the confidence to step forward when others stepped back. It meant being willing to help, protect, and serve regardless of the circumstances. Those qualities would later prove invaluable in my career choices. I realized that the same fearlessness that guided me as a child naturally led me toward careers in public service. Serving as a firefighter and later as a police officer required courage, quick decision making, and a commitment to helping others, often during some of the most difficult moments of their lives. Looking back, it is clear that God was preparing me from an early age for a life of service. The lessons I learned as a young boy taught me that courage is not the absence of fear. Courage is moving forward despite fear. That mindset not only shaped my childhood, but it also helped shape the man I would become.

CHAPTER FIVE
Lessons From Mississippi

Sometimes my mother would wake us up in the middle of the night and ask if we wanted to go to Mississippi. That was her hometown. Those trips were always an adventure. My mother came from a large family. She had eleven aunts and uncles. When we arrived in Mississippi there were always relatives everywhere. But before we got there, she gave us strict instructions. Do not look white people in the eyes when you talk to them. Say yes sir. Say no sir. Speak respectfully. Those rules were not about manners. They were about survival. The South during those years was a different world. Words and eye contact could be taken as disrespect. And disrespect could lead to trouble.

When we visited Mississippi, I met my grandmother and great grandmother. Looking back now, I realize how close history really was. My father was born in 1915. That means the people who raised him were only one or two generations removed from slavery. History was not something in a book. It was sitting right there on the front porch. As a boy I did not ask enough questions. I was too busy running around playing and enjoying being young. But later in life I realized that those elders carried stories that should have been written down. Wisdom does not always shout. Sometimes it sits quietly on a porch waiting for someone to ask the right question. I wish I had spent more time talking with my parents, grandparents, and other elders about what life was really like growing up in Mississippi during segregation. I wish I had asked them what challenges they faced, what sacrifices they made, and how they found the strength to persevere during some of the most difficult times in our nation's history.

At the time, I did not fully appreciate that I was surrounded by living history. I realize just how valuable those conversations would have been. Now I understand how important it is to know your history and to preserve the stories of those who came before you. Our ancestors endured unimaginable hardships, yet they continued to push forward in hopes that future generations would have opportunities they never had. Many of the freedoms and opportunities we enjoy today came at a great cost. Things that some people take for granted, such as the right to vote, equal rights under the law, attending integrated schools, pursuing careers without barriers, and even witnessing the election of our nation's first Black president, were made possible because countless men and women fought, sacrificed, and, in some cases, gave their lives for those rights. Knowing our history gives us a greater appreciation for the sacrifices that were made on our behalf. It reminds us that progress did not happen overnight and that each generation has a responsibility to learn from the past, honor those who came before us, and continue striving to leave the world better for those who will follow.

CHAPTER SIX

Becoming Somebody

I attended Dunbar Grade School until the fourth grade. Later I transferred to Laclede Grade School. At that time there were only three Black students. Joe. Fred. And Francis. That was it. Looking back now, I realize the situation could have been much more difficult than it was. But at the time I simply focused on school and activities. By seventh grade more Black students started attending the school. Things slowly began to change. During my eighth-grade year I was elected captain of the patrol boys. I was also the supply monitor and hall monitor. Truth be told I seemed to have every responsibility in the school except sitting quietly in class.

During that time, I also stayed active outside of work. I played football for the fire department, and that was something I really enjoyed. It kept me sharp and connected with the men I worked alongside. Boxing was another sport I took seriously. I was good at it too. It taught me discipline, how to stay focused, and how to handle pressure. That simple habit helped shape me more than I realized. It built awareness. It built discipline. It gave me a mindset that said there's always more to learn, always more to understand. Sometimes becoming somebody doesn't start with something big. I also played softball and basketball. Our team won the city championship. I even received a trophy for softball. I was proud of that trophy. Sports gave young men like me something important. Confidence. Discipline. Purpose. My uncle Charlie Vaughn was a two-time Missouri State heavyweight boxing champion. He even sparred with Sonny Liston. That was a big deal. When you grow up around men like that, you begin to believe that maybe you can become something too.

I also met Curt Flood and Bob Gibson from the St. Louis Cardinals. Curt Flood surprised me. He was not much taller than I was at thirteen years old. That moment taught me something important. Greatness does not always look the way you expect it to look. Sometimes the people who make history look just like the rest of us. In January of 1967, my only son was born, Gilbert O. Vaughn. I still remember that moment clearly. There is something about holding your child for the first time that changes the way you see the world. It gives you a different kind of responsibility. His mother's name is Loretta, and at that time, I was stepping into adulthood whether I was fully ready or not.

I got married at the age of nineteen. Looking back now, I can say honestly that I was too young. At that age, you think you understand life, but you are still learning who you are. Marriage is a serious commitment, and it takes more than just good intentions to make it work. Still, those experiences were part of my journey. Becoming a father at a young age forced me to grow up quickly. It made me think differently about responsibility, about providing, and about the kind of man I wanted to become. Getting married at nineteen added another layer to that reality. At that age, you are still learning who you are. You are still figuring things out. And trying to build a life with someone else while doing that can be challenging. But even those challenges teach you something. They teach you about responsibility. They teach you about commitment. They teach you about growth.

Becoming a father at a young age added another layer to that process. Responsibility became more immediate. Decisions began to carry more weight. The focus shifted toward providing and making sure that the right steps were taken moving forward. That period of life was a transition. Moving from being guided to taking on responsibility. Learning through experience. Adjusting to new expectations. Each part contributed to becoming more aware of what it meant to grow into adulthood.

I learned in life is that major decisions made when you are young can have a lasting impact on your future. When we are young, we often believe we have all the answers. We sometimes make decisions based on emotions, peer pressure, pride, or simply because we do not fully understand the consequences of our choices. The truth is that every decision matters. The friends we choose, the paths we take, the opportunities we pursue, and even the mistakes we make can shape the course of our lives for years to come. That is why it is important for young people to seek wisdom, listen to those who have traveled the road before them, and think carefully before making life changing decisions.

At the same time, I have learned that life should be lived without regrets. We cannot spend our lives looking backward, wishing we had done things differently. Every challenge, disappointment, setback, and mistake carries with it a lesson. Those experiences help shape our character, strengthen our faith, and prepare us for what lies ahead. As I reflect on my own journey, I realize that some of life's greatest lessons came through difficult times. While I may not have understood it then, those experiences taught me perseverance, humility, compassion, and resilience. They also provided stories and wisdom that I can now pass on to my children, grandchildren, and future generations.

Our experiences, both good and bad, become part of our legacy. By sharing our stories, we give future generations the benefit of our successes, our failures, and the lessons we learned along the way. Hopefully, they can learn from our experiences and be inspired to make wise decisions while creating their own meaningful journey through life. Every part of this chapter of my life, even the parts that were not perfect, contributed to who I became. Nothing was wasted. Each experience added something. Each moment pushed me forward. Even when I did not fully understand it at the time.

As I moved through school, I began to understand that being involved mattered. Taking on responsibilities, even small ones, created a sense of direction. It gave structure to my day and helped me stay focused. Being chosen for different roles at school was not something I took lightly. It meant that someone saw potential and trusted me to handle responsibility. That kind of trust encourages you to take things more seriously. Staying active in sports also contributed to that growth. Practice required consistency. Games required focus. Working with a team required cooperation. Each part added something to how I approached challenges. There is also a level of discipline that comes from staying busy in the right way. It keeps your attention on productive activities. It reduces distractions that might pull you in a different direction. Seeing successful individuals up close created a different kind of motivation. When you meet people who have achieved something significant, it changes how you think about what is possible. It removes the idea that success is out of reach.

CHAPTER SEVEN

Looking Beyond St. Louis

As I got older, I began realizing there was a big world outside the neighborhoods I had grown up in. When you are young, the streets around your home feel like the center of everything. But eventually curiosity starts pulling you beyond those familiar corners. Travel has a way of changing how you see life. I was fortunate enough to see parts of the world that many people never get the chance to see. Over the years I traveled from Alaska all the way to South Africa. Each place had its own personality. Alaska felt wild and untouched, like the land still belonged more to nature than to people. The air was different there. Crisp and quiet. It made you feel small in the best possible way.

South Africa was something else entirely. One of the most unforgettable experiences of my life was staying in the jungle in Kruger Park. If you have never been somewhere like that, it is hard to explain what it feels like. At night the jungle is alive. You hear sounds everywhere. Animals moving in the distance. Birds calling out. Branches cracking. It reminds you that human beings are not the only creatures living on this planet. Being there made me realize how big the world really is.

I also traveled to Rome where the Pope lives. Standing in a city that old makes you think about time in a different way. Buildings there have been standing for hundreds and sometimes thousands of years. History surrounds you in every direction. When you grow up in a country like the United States, where most things are relatively new, places like Rome make you realize just how much has happened in the world long before you arrived. Travel does something important for the mind. It opens it. You begin to see that every place has its own struggles and its own beauty. But everywhere you go, people are trying to do the same basic thing. They are trying to build a life. They are trying to protect their families. They are trying to find some meaning in the time they have here. That realization stayed with me for the rest of my life.

One of the greatest gifts a person can give themselves is the opportunity to travel and experience the world through a different lens. Traveling allows you to step outside of your comfort zone and see that there is a big world beyond the neighborhood or city where you were raised. I came to appreciate the value of traveling. Each new place, culture, and experience taught me something valuable. It broadened my perspective and helped me understand that people may live differently, speak differently, worship differently, and view life differently, yet we all share many of the same hopes, dreams, and desires. Traveling also teaches humility. It reminds us that our way is not the only way and that there is much we can learn from others. It challenges preconceived notions, breaks down stereotypes, and encourages us to become more open minded and compassionate.

Seeing the world through a different lens allows us to appreciate diversity and recognize the beauty that exists in people from all walks of life. Some of life's greatest lessons are not learned in a classroom, but through experiences, conversations, and relationships built while traveling. I encourage future generations to travel whenever possible. Explore new places, meet new people, and embrace new experiences. The world has much to teach us, and every journey has the potential to leave us wiser, more grateful, and better prepared to understand both ourselves and others.

CHAPTER EIGHT

Los Angeles and the Road Home

Before I officially started my career in public service, I spent some time in Los Angeles, California. That was a big change from St. Louis. Los Angeles had a completely different energy. The weather was different. The pace of life was different. Everything seemed bigger and louder. I stayed there for about six months with a man named Mac. Mac was a World War II veteran. He was my mother's cousin that lived through experiences most people could only imagine. During the war he had seen things that stayed with him for the rest of his life. Mac had written a book about his experiences during the war, and I still have that book today. Living with him was an education all by itself. When someone who has been through a world war sits down and tells you stories, you listen.

Those conversations gave me a deeper appreciation for what that generation endured. They had faced dangers that most of us will never understand. Los Angeles was exciting, but something inside me knew I was not meant to stay there forever. Sometimes life pulls you back to where your purpose is waiting. For me, that place was St. Louis. Eventually I returned home because I knew what I wanted to do. I wanted to serve. There have been seasons in my life when I wanted nothing more than to keep moving forward, only to discover that life had other plans. I did not always understand why certain doors closed or why unexpected setbacks occurred. With time, however, I came to realize that some delays carry valuable lessons. When you are young, you often believe that every detour is an obstacle standing in your way. Some detours are actually guiding you in the right direction.

Recognizing that life's interruptions are not always meant to discourage us. Sometimes they are meant to slow us down long enough for us to see what truly matters. There were many moments throughout my journey when circumstances forced me to pause, reflect, and reevaluate my direction. Those moments proved to be some of the most important in my life. Not everything in life unfolds according to our plans. In fact, some of life's greatest lessons emerge during the times when our plans are unexpectedly changed.

Chapter Nine

Choosing the Uniform

When I returned to St. Louis, I moved to Lucas Hunt in a community called Velda Village. That is where I began taking the first real steps toward my career. I submitted my application to the St. Louis Police Department and was accepted into the police academy. The training was demanding, but it was also exciting. For the first time I was stepping into a role where I could truly serve the community. I graduated from the police academy in May of 1973.

But something unexpected happened shortly before graduation. The fire department called me. Now the truth is I had always wanted to be a firefighter. But at that moment I was already deep into the police academy and only had about one month left before finishing. So, I told them the truth. I said I really wanted to be a firefighter, but I only needed one more month to complete the police academy. Then I asked them something I did not expect them to agree to. I asked if they would place me back on the list for firefighters once I graduated.

To be honest, I did not think they would. But they did. Sometimes life works in ways you do not expect. At that time there were nearly fifteen hundred firefighters in the department. Only about eighty of them were Black. I would soon become one of them. Looking back now, that decision changed the direction of my entire life. Pursuing a career as a firefighter was not as simple as filling out an application and waiting for a phone call. The process was demanding, competitive, and required a great deal of patience and perseverance. From the very beginning, I understood that if I truly wanted to serve my community as a firefighter, I would have to be willing to put in the work.

The application process itself was challenging. There were written examinations, physical fitness requirements, background checks, interviews, and long periods of waiting. At times, the process could be frustrating and discouraging. There were moments when it seemed as though progress was moving slowly, and there was no guarantee of success. Preparing for the physical portion of the process required discipline and determination. A firefighter must be physically and mentally prepared to respond to emergencies at a moment's notice. I knew that people's lives could one day depend on my ability to perform under pressure, so I took the responsibility seriously.

NEIL J. SVETANICS
FIRE CHIEF

ST. LOUIS FIRE DEPARTMENT
FIRE ACADEMY
DEPARTMENT OF PUBLIC SAFETY
1421 N. JEFFERSON
ST. LOUIS, MISSOURI 63106
(314) 289-1920

VINCENT C. SCHOEMEHL, JR.
MAYOR

WILLIAM J. KUEHLING
DIRECTOR OF PUBLIC SAFETY

DAVID WEMAN
BATTALION CHIEF

May 11, 1993

Captain Gilbert Vaughn
Engine Company #10 A

Captain Vaughn,

It is my pleasure to acknowledge and comment upon the manner in which you distinguished yourself during heroic action in the rescue of a victim from a residential fire on March 4, 1993 at 2914 Euclid.

Your quick action reflects favorably upon the efficiency of this Department and upon your ability as a member of the St. Louis Fire Department.

I extend you sincere thanks for a job well done.

Congratulations!

Sincerely,

Neil Svetanics
Fire Chief

NS/ej
cc: files

What I learned during the application process was that perseverance is often the difference between success and failure. Many people begin the journey, but not everyone remains committed when obstacles arise. I was determined not to give up. I believed that if this was the path meant for me, then every challenge along the way was simply preparing me for the responsibilities that lay ahead. The difficulties associated with becoming a firefighter taught me valuable lessons about patience, resilience, and commitment. Those lessons not only helped me earn the opportunity to serve, but they also stayed with me throughout my career and in other areas of my life.

CHAPTER TEN

The Police Years

Working as a police officer teaches you things that most people never see. You respond to calls at all hours of the day and night. Sometimes the calls are routine. Sometimes they turn into something much more serious. One call that stayed with me started out simple. We received a report about a man sleeping in a car. When my partner and I arrived, the car was sitting quietly along the street. At first nothing seemed unusual. But when I looked inside the vehicle, I saw something that did not feel right.

There was a body lying in the back seat. Someone had tried to cover it with trash bags. In this line of work, you learn quickly that situations can change in an instant. One moment you think you are responding to something minor. The next moment you are standing in the middle of a crime scene. Moments like that remind you that the world has both good and bad in it. It takes all kinds of people to make up this world. Some good. Some not so good. The police years introduced me to a side of life that many people never have to face directly. When you wear that uniform, you are stepping into situations that are often unpredictable. You do not always know what you are walking into. You receive a call, you respond, and you deal with whatever is waiting for you on the other side.

That uncertainty becomes part of the job. At first, you may try to prepare yourself for every possible situation. But over time, you realize that no amount of preparation can cover everything. Life does not work that way. Each call is different. Each situation carries its own set of circumstances. And you learn to adjust in real time. The call about the man in the car is a perfect example of that. It started as something routine. Something simple. But it quickly became something else entirely. That moment stays with you because it shifts your understanding.

You begin to realize that what you see on the surface is not always the full story. You begin to look closer. Pay attention more. Trust your instincts. Those experiences also change how you see people. You begin to understand that everyone is carrying something. Some people are dealing with situations you can see. Others are dealing with things you cannot. But either way, you learn that life is not always as straightforward as it appears. Working as a police officer also teaches you control. Control of your emotions. Control of your reactions. Because in certain situations, how you respond matters just as much as what you are responding to. You cannot allow panic to take over. You cannot allow fear to control your actions. You have to remain steady. Even when things are not. Those years taught me a lot about awareness, discipline, and responsibility. Lessons that would carry into every part of my life moving forward.

Working in law enforcement exposes you to situations that most people never encounter. Each call presents a different set of circumstances, and you quickly learn that no two situations are exactly the same. Routine calls can shift without warning. What starts as something minor can become serious within moments. That unpredictability requires constant awareness and readiness. You also begin to understand how people respond under pressure. Some remain calm. Others react emotionally. Each situation requires a different approach, and part of the job is learning how to adjust in real time.

The experience with the vehicle showed how quickly a situation can change. What appeared to be a simple call revealed something far more serious. Moments like that reinforce the need to stay alert and observant at all times. Over time, you develop instincts that guide your actions. You begin to notice details that others might overlook. That awareness becomes a critical part of how you operate. The job also provides insight into different aspects of society. You see a wide range of situations, from everyday issues to more complex challenges. That exposure creates a broader understanding of how people live and the difficulties they may face. Working in that environment builds resilience. It requires you to remain steady, even when faced with difficult circumstances. That steadiness becomes part of how you approach both the job and life outside of it.

Not every call during my years in public service was dramatic or action packed, but each one left an impression. One call that I will never forget involved a request from the police department to conduct a family welfare check on a resident in the community.

Unfortunately, when we arrived, we discovered that the individual had passed away. Due to circumstances beyond our control, I had to remain on the scene for nearly eight hours while waiting for the coroner to arrive and transport the body. I remember this particular incident because the gentleman was well known and respected in the community. In fact, a street was named in his honor, a testament to the impact he had made during his lifetime.

Now, I have to admit that spending eight hours alone with a deceased individual can play tricks on your mind. To pass the time, I found myself walking back and forth, whistling, and doing just about anything I could to stay occupied. The truth is, deep down inside, I was also keeping a close eye on things because I wanted to make absolutely certain that the body did not decide to move! Of course, the gentleman remained right where he was, but after several hours, every creak, shadow, and unfamiliar noise seemed amplified. Looking back, I can laugh about it now, but at the time, I was not taking any chances. I had seen a lot during my career, but I was not interested in witnessing a miracle of that kind.

Chapter Eleven

The Firefighter I Wanted to Be

Becoming a firefighter was something I had wanted for a long time. When the opportunity finally came, I knew I had found my place. Firefighting is not just about putting out fires. It is about protecting people during some of the worst moments of their lives. It is about walking into danger while everyone else is trying to get out. When I joined the department there were very few Black firefighters. That meant we often had to prove ourselves more than once. But hard work earns respect eventually. You learn the job. You show up when it matters. And over time people begin to see the kind of person you are. The firehouse becomes its own kind of family. You depend on the people beside you. Because when you enter a burning building, trust is not optional. It is necessary.

There were moments when I felt the pressure of having to work twice as hard to prove that I belonged. I understood that my performance would not only reflect on me as an individual, but, in many ways, on other African Americans who would come after me. That was a responsibility I did not take lightly. Being one of the few meant that there were not many people who looked like me or shared similar life experiences. There were times when I faced challenges, skepticism, and barriers that others may not have fully understood. However, rather than allowing those experiences to discourage me, I used them as motivation to excel.

I recognized that I was standing on the shoulders of men and women who had fought for the opportunity for African Americans to serve in professions that were once closed to us. Their sacrifices opened doors that previous generations could only dream about walking through. Because of them, I was afforded the opportunity to serve my community in a profession that I loved.

Over time, I came to appreciate that representation matters. Seeing African Americans in positions of service and leadership sends a powerful message to young people that they, too, can pursue careers that may once have seemed out of reach. I hoped that by serving with integrity, professionalism, and dedication, I could help pave the way for those who would follow. The fire service was the brotherhood that developed among the men and women I served alongside. While we all came from different backgrounds, worked different shifts, and had different life experiences, the firehouse had a unique way of bringing people together. Over time, my fellow firefighters became much more than coworkers; they became family.

There is something special about working in a profession where you literally place your life in the hands of others. When the alarm sounds, there is no time for hesitation. You have to trust that the person standing beside you is trained, prepared, and committed to bringing everyone home safely. That kind of trust cannot be manufactured. It is earned through long hours, shared experiences, and facing challenges together.

The firehouse was more than a workplace. It became a second home. We celebrated birthdays, holidays, promotions, and personal milestones together. We shared meals, laughter, stories, and sometimes disagreements. We also stood together during difficult times, supporting one another through personal losses, tragedies, and the emotional toll that often accompanies a career in public service. Many people see firefighters responding to emergencies, but what they do not always see are the countless hours spent together between calls. Those moments helped build strong bonds and lasting friendships. We learned about one another's families, encouraged one another during hard times, and developed a level of camaraderie that extended far beyond the walls of the fire station.

Having that support system was important because the nature of the job exposed us to situations that most people never experience. There were calls that stayed with us long after the sirens were silenced. During those moments, it was comforting to know that the people around you understood exactly what you were feeling because they had experienced it alongside you. Some of my fondest memories from the fire service are not tied to a particular fire or emergency, but to the relationships that were formed along the way. The friendships I built in the fire department lasted long after retirement because we were more than a team. We were family, united by a shared commitment to serve others and by experiences that only we could truly understand.

There were plenty of serious moments during my years in the fire department, but there were also a lot of laughs. One call that still makes me smile involved my fellow firefighter, Eddie Lee. We responded to a structure fire, and before entering the building, I told Eddie to wait and let me go in first. Older buildings can be unpredictable, and I wanted to make sure the floor was stable before anyone else came in. I made it inside without any problems and signaled for Eddie to follow. The moment he stepped into the building, the floor gave way beneath him. In the blink of an eye, Eddie disappeared through a hole in the floor. The funny thing about it was that even though I went in first, Eddie somehow managed to beat me to the bottom.

Thankfully, he was not seriously injured, but once we knew he was okay, there was no way we were going to let him forget it. For years afterward, whenever the story came up, someone would always joke that Eddie was just trying to find a faster way downstairs. Firefighting can be physically and emotionally demanding, so moments like these were important. Laughter helped ease the stress and brought us closer together as a team. Even now, many years later, that incident still brings a smile to my face. I am proud not only of the career I built, but also of the barriers that were broken along the way. My journey taught me that being "the only one" or "one of the few" should never discourage anyone from pursuing their dreams. Sometimes, being first simply means that you have been called to open the door for others.

CHAPTER TWELVE

The Calls You Never Forget

Some calls stay with you forever. One of the first fire deaths I experienced happened when a mentally challenged young man set his own house on fire. He had argued with his brother and wanted to scare him. His plan was to set the fire and then rescue the house so he would look like a hero. But fire does not follow your plans. By the time we arrived the flames were already spreading. Smoke filled the house as we entered to search for anyone still inside. That is when we found his brother. He was lying on the stairway. Dead. Just like that. Moments like that teach you something about life very quickly. Anger can last a few minutes. But the consequences can last forever.

Some of my most memorable calls had nothing to do with fighting fires. In fact, a few of them provided enough laughter to last a lifetime. One afternoon, we received a call from the police department from a woman who was in complete distress because a squirrel had somehow found its way into her house. She was determined to have it removed immediately. When I arrived, I figured this would be a quick and easy call. I couldn't have been more wrong. That squirrel had no plans of cooperating. Every time I thought I had it trapped, it would race across the room, sending both the homeowner and me in the opposite direction. Before long, the squirrel had us running laps throughout the entire house. At one point, we were both yelling and jumping every time the squirrel changed course. Looking back, I am still not sure who was more afraid.

After spending what felt like an eternity chasing that little creature, I finally asked the homeowner, "Would you like me to just shoot it?" She quickly replied, "No!

There would be blood everywhere!" Realizing that neither one of us was winning this battle, we contacted Animal Control for advice. Their recommendation was simple: place an apple near an open window and let nature take its course.

Surprisingly, it worked. After causing complete chaos throughout the house, the squirrel eventually made its way toward the apple and escaped through the window. Even now, years later, I can't help but laugh about that day. Firefighters are trained to handle dangerous situations, but on that particular call, a single squirrel managed to outsmart all of us.

CHAPTER THIRTEEN

The Bicycle on the Hill

One call from my years on the fire department has stayed with me for the rest of my life. A young man was riding his ten-speed bicycle down a very steep hill. Anyone who has ever ridden a bicycle downhill knows how fast you can pick up speed when gravity takes over. Somewhere on that hill his brakes failed. Once that happened, he had no way to stop. The bicycle kept gaining speed until he reached the bottom of the hill where a car was passing through the intersection. He crashed directly into it. The impact knocked him under the vehicle and the car rolled on top of him. When we arrived on the scene, people were already standing around the car in shock. Nobody was moving. Nobody knew what to do.

You could see the fear on their faces. We had to bring equipment to jack the car up off of him. Every firefighter there understood the situation before the car even lifted. Some accidents leave very little hope. But we still had a job to do. Moments like that stay with you because you realize how fragile life really is. One mechanical failure. One moment of bad timing. One second. And everything changes.

Serving in public service teaches you very quickly that life is not always fair. No amount of training can fully prepare you for the heartbreak, loss, and tragedy you will encounter while serving others. There were calls that ended in celebration and relief, but there were also calls that ended in sorrow. Those were the calls that often stayed with you long after your shift had ended. One of the hardest realities of the job was understanding that despite your best efforts, you cannot save everyone. As first responders, we arrive hoping to make a difference, to provide comfort, and, whenever possible, to save lives. Yet there are times when circumstances are beyond anyone's control. Accepting that reality is not easy.

Learning how to cope with tragedy became an important part of surviving the profession. For many of us, the firehouse became a place where we could lean on one another. The people I served beside understood the emotional weight of the job because they had carried it themselves. We supported one another, shared stories, and found strength in our common experiences. I also discovered the importance of appreciating life and not taking a single day for granted. Witnessing tragedy on a regular basis has a way of changing your perspective.

You begin to value family more, cherish friendships, and recognize that tomorrow is never promised.

Humor played an important role as well. While outsiders may not always understand it, laughter often helped us process difficult situations and release some of the stress that came with the job. It was one of the ways we managed to continue serving without allowing the sadness we witnessed to consume us. Public service taught me many lessons, but perhaps the greatest was this: life is precious, and we should make the most of the time we have with the people we love. No one is guaranteed tomorrow, which is why it is so important to live with purpose, extend grace to others, and never leave important words unsaid.

Chapter Fourteen

The Fire with the Missing Child

Another call that I will never forget involved a fire in a building where a child was reported missing. When the call came in, we responded quickly and began fighting the fire. Flames were moving through the building, but eventually we got them under control. At first it seemed like everyone had made it out safely. Then the mother arrived. She was frantic. She kept repeating the same words over and over again. "My son is still inside." That is the moment every firefighter dreads. When someone tells you there is still a child inside a burning building, the entire operation changes instantly. We began searching the house again. Room by room. Corner by corner.

Smoke damage makes it difficult to see anything clearly. Every step you take feels uncertain. Eventually we found him. He was behind the gas stove. The boy had tried to hide from the fire. But the smoke had reached him first. Those are the moments that weigh on you long after the fire is out. People often thank firefighters for their bravery. But what stays with you are the moments when you wish you had arrived just a few minutes earlier.

Many people would be surprised to learn just how different the fire service was when I first joined the department. Back then, we did not have many of the comforts that firefighters enjoy today. There was no air conditioning in the firehouse and very little heat during the winter months. The philosophy at the time was that firefighters should remain accustomed to the outdoor elements. Many believed that sleeping in cooler temperatures and spending more time in the open air would help regulate the body's temperature and better prepare firefighters for the demands of the job.

As a result, many of us slept in our clothes, always ready to respond at a moment's notice. It was not unusual to wake up in the middle of the night, jump into action, and head straight to a call. The fire trucks were different as well. We rode what was known as an "open-air cab." Unlike today's enclosed fire apparatus, portions of the truck were exposed to the elements. Three firefighters would often ride on the back step facing backward. During the colder months, we would turn our backs to the wind in an effort to keep the freezing air from hitting us directly in the face. Needless to say, winter rides to a fire scene could be quite an experience.

Looking back, those conditions may sound harsh by today's standards, but at the time, it was simply part of the job. We did not complain because we did not know any different. In many ways, those experiences helped build resilience, toughness, and camaraderie among the firefighters. We learned to adapt, rely on one another, and take pride in doing the job regardless of the conditions. Today's firefighters benefit from significant advancements in equipment, technology, and safety measures, and rightly so. However, there is something special about remembering the way things used to be. Those experiences are part of the history of the fire service and a reminder of how much the profession has evolved over the years.

CHAPTER FIFTEEN

Death Up Close

Working in emergency services changes how you see life. When you respond to enough calls involving death, you begin to understand something many people spend their whole lives avoiding. Life is temporary. One call during my time as a police officer involved a man believed to be having a heart attack. When we arrived, he was lying in bed talking to us. He seemed calm. He told us he would be alright. We started CPR while waiting for medical assistance. But at that time, we did not realize he should have been moved to the floor. One moment he was speaking. The next moment he was gone. Just like that. Death can arrive quietly in the middle of an ordinary moment. Experiences like that change the way you live your life. You begin to appreciate the simple things. A conversation. A quiet day. The chance to wake up tomorrow. Because none of those things are guaranteed.

After spending a lifetime serving as both a firefighter and police officer, I came to understand something that many people do not fully appreciate until much later in life: our time here is limited. There is a saying that I have repeated for years, usually followed by a laugh: "Don't take life so seriously, because you're not getting out alive." While the statement may sound humorous, there is a deeper meaning behind it. Working in public service exposed me to the unpredictable nature of life. I saw firsthand how quickly circumstances could change. Families could begin their day expecting an ordinary morning, only to find themselves facing unimaginable loss by the end of the day. Experiences like those have a way of changing your outlook.

Recognizing that life is temporary forces you to think differently about what truly matters. You begin to place less importance on material possessions and more importance on relationships. You realize that arguments, grudges, and petty disagreements are rarely worth sacrificing precious time with the people you love. Understanding life's temporary nature also encourages us to pursue our dreams, take meaningful risks, and create memories while we can. Too many people spend their lives waiting for the perfect time to travel, start a business, mend a relationship, or simply enjoy the present moment. Unfortunately, the perfect time does not always come.

None of us know how much time we have. For that reason, I believe we should make the most of each day. Laugh often. Forgive freely. Tell people you love them.

Take the trip. Chase the dream. Create memories that will outlive you. In the end, our legacy will not be defined by what we owned, but by how we treated others, the lives we impacted, and the love we leave behind.

Chapter Sixteen

Looking Back at the Road

The firehouse becomes its own kind of family. Firefighters spend long hours together. You eat together. You train together. You trust each other with your lives. When the alarm sounds and the trucks roll out, you know the men beside you are the ones who will help you make it back. That kind of bond cannot be faked.

During those years the department still had very few Black firefighters. There were challenges that came with that reality. But hard work and professionalism speak louder than anything else. If you know your job and do it well, people eventually respect that. The firehouse taught me discipline. It also taught me humility. Because fire does not care who you are. When you walk into a burning building, everyone is equal in the face of danger.

Now that I have lived many years, I sometimes sit and think about the path life took me on. A boy born in St. Louis in 1947. Growing up on Thomas Street. Watching horses pull rag carts through the alley. Waiting for a white horse that never arrived. Seeing the country change through the Civil Rights movement. Traveling across the world from Alaska to Africa. Serving as both a police officer and a firefighter.

Witnessing the best and worst of human nature. Life has a way of surprising you. You start out walking one road and suddenly another door opens. If there is one thing I have learned, it is that life cannot be fully planned. Sometimes you just have to step forward and see where the road leads.

CHAPTER SEVENTEEN

What Life Taught Me

At seventy-eight years old, I have learned a few things worth sharing. First, life moves faster than you think. One day you are a child watching your father build a walkway. The next day you are the old man telling the story. Second, people matter more than things. Houses disappear. Neighborhoods change. But the people who shared those moments with you remain part of your story forever. Third, do not take life too seriously. Nobody gets out alive anyway.

You might as well laugh when you can. Fourth, courage matters. My mother taught me that when she sent us back into that grocery store. Fear will stop you from doing many things in life. But courage moves you forward. And finally, remember this. Every day you wake up is another opportunity. Another chance to do something good. Another chance to help someone. Another chance to live with purpose.

When you reach this stage in life, lessons begin to feel less like ideas and more like truths you have lived through. Time is one of the first things that becomes clear. When you are young, it feels like there is plenty of it. You think in terms of years ahead. Later, you begin to think in terms of moments behind you. That shift changes how you see everything. It makes you more aware of how quickly seasons pass and how important it is to be present while you are in them.

The importance of people becomes even clearer over time. You start to understand that the things you once thought mattered do not hold the same weight. Possessions come and go. Places change. But the relationships you build and the people you share life with leave a lasting mark. Those connections carry meaning long after everything else has shifted.

Humor also becomes more important than you might expect. Life brings enough serious moments on its own. Learning to laugh, even during difficult times, gives you balance. It allows you to move through challenges without

People sometimes ask what it means to be a hero. Movies show heroes as larger than life figures who perform incredible acts. But real heroism often looks much simpler than that. A hero is someone who shows up when they are needed. Someone who stands firm when things become difficult. Someone who chooses service over comfort. I never considered myself famous. I was not rich. But I lived a life filled with experiences that shaped who I became. I served my community. I protected people when they needed help. I witnessed history changing around me.

And I learned lessons that I hope others can carry forward. If my story teaches anything, it is this. Ordinary people can live extraordinary lives. You do not have to be famous. You do not have to be wealthy. You only have to live with courage, honesty, and purpose. If you do that, you have already become something important. Maybe even a hero.

CHAPTER EIGHTEEN

The Neighborhood That Raised Me

When people talk about where they come from, they often mention the city or the state. But for most of us, the place that really raises us is a neighborhood. A neighborhood has its own character. It has its own sounds. It has its own way of teaching you how the world works. Thomas Street in St. Louis was the place where my understanding of life first began to form. The houses stood close together, and the alleys behind them were almost like another street of their own. Children played there, neighbors talked there, and the rag men with their horses traveled through those alleys collecting whatever it was they were collecting.

Back then, the sound of horses' hooves hitting the pavement was normal. You could hear them coming long before they appeared around the corner. Life moved slower in those days. People knew their neighbors. Adults looked out for the children on the block, even if those children were not their own. If someone's mother saw you doing something you were not supposed to be doing, she might correct you right there on the spot. And when you got home, your own parents would probably correct you again. Discipline was not considered cruel. It was considered necessary. Looking back now, I realize that those neighborhoods were filled with lessons that could not be taught in classrooms. You learned respect. You learned responsibility. You learned that your actions affected the people around you. Those early lessons stayed with me long after the neighborhood itself had changed.

Our family was not wealthy. But we had something just as valuable. We had each other. My father, A.C. Vaughn, believed in working hard and doing things the right way. Watching him build that small brick walkway when I was a boy may not seem like an important memory to someone else, but it meant something to me. It showed me the pride a man can take in honest work. He did not rush. He placed each brick carefully. Sometimes the simplest moments end up teaching the biggest lessons. My mother, Effie Vaughn, was a strong woman who carried a lot of responsibility on her shoulders. Raising children while working and keeping a household running is not easy, especially during difficult times. But she managed it.

She expected us to behave properly. She expected us to work hard. And she expected us to treat people with respect. Those expectations shaped the kind of men my brother and I would eventually become. Family was not just something you talked about back then. Family meant responsibility. When my great uncle James Visor was injured as a child after being kicked in the head by a mule, his life changed forever. But the family did not abandon him. Different relatives took turns caring for him throughout his life. He was part of the family, and family takes care of its own. That was simply the way things were done.

Chapter Nineteen
The World Was Changing

The America I grew up in looked very different from the America we see today. During the 1950s and 1960s, the country was going through major changes. The Civil Rights Movement was challenging long standing systems that had treated Black Americans unfairly for generations. At the time, many of us did not fully understand how historic those moments would become. We were simply living through them. But looking back now, I realize how much courage it took for many people to stand up and demand equal treatment. The world does not change overnight. It changes because individuals decide they are no longer willing to accept injustice. Sometimes those decisions come with risks. But progress rarely happens without someone being willing to step forward first. Growing up during those years taught me something important. Change is possible. But it requires patience, courage, and persistence.

Living through a period of change is different from reading about it later. At the time, it does not always feel historic. It feels like everyday life. People going to work. People raising families. People dealing with what is in front of them. But underneath that, something bigger is happening. Shifts in thinking. Shifts in opportunity. Shifts in what people are willing to accept. As a young person, you may not fully grasp the weight of those changes. You just experience them. You see things evolving. You notice differences. But the full meaning often comes later.

Looking back now, it is clear how much courage it took for people to push forward during that time. To challenge systems. To step into spaces where they were not always welcomed. To stand firm in the face of resistance. That kind of courage moves things forward. It opens doors. It creates opportunities for the next generation. And even if you are not directly involved in those moments, you are still affected by them.

They shape the environment you grow up in. They influence what becomes possible. That period of change left a lasting impact. Not just on the country. But on individuals who lived through it. It showed that progress does not happen by accident. It happens through persistence. Through effort. Through people deciding that things can be different. Change does not always feel significant while it is happening. Daily life continues, routines stay in place, and people focus on what is directly in front of them. It is only later that the full impact becomes clear. During that period, there were noticeable shifts in how people moved, where they went, and what opportunities were available. Some changes were gradual, while others felt more immediate.

Awareness of those shifts developed over time. You began to notice differences in access, in behavior, and in how certain spaces were approached. Those observations created a broader understanding of what was taking place. The presence of change also introduced uncertainty. Not everything was predictable, and not every outcome was clear. That required patience and the ability to adapt. At the same time, there was progress. New opportunities began to appear, even if they were limited at first. Each step forward contributed to a larger movement. Living through that period created a perspective that extends beyond individual experience. It showed that change is possible, but it requires time, effort, and persistence.

CHAPTER TWENTY

What Travel Teaches You

Travel has a way of expanding your understanding of the world. When you leave the place where you grew up and see other countries, other cultures, and other ways of living, it forces you to realize that your own experience is only one small piece of a much larger picture. When I visited Africa and spent time in Kruger Park, I experienced a different kind of environment than anything I had known before. The jungle has its own rhythm. During the day the sunlight filters through the trees and everything feels alive. But at night the jungle becomes something entirely different. You hear animals moving in the darkness.

You hear sounds that you cannot always identify. It reminds you that nature operates according to its own rules. Standing in a place like that makes you realize how powerful the natural world truly is. In Rome, the experience was different but just as meaningful. The buildings and streets carry centuries of history. You walk through places where countless people have lived their lives long before you ever arrived. Travel does something important. It humbles you. It reminds you that the world is much bigger than your own personal story.

Serving as a police officer and firefighter comes with a heavy responsibility. People call you when they are facing some of the worst moments of their lives. They expect you to arrive with solutions. They expect you to stay calm when everything around them feels chaotic. That kind of responsibility cannot be taken lightly. Training prepares you for many situations. But some moments cannot truly be prepared for. When you respond to accidents, fires, and emergencies, you are often seeing people at their most vulnerable. You witness grief. You witness fear. You witness loss. But you also witness courage. You see neighbors helping neighbors. You see strangers risking their safety to help someone they have never met. Those moments remind you that even in difficult times, humanity still has the ability to show compassion.

What people don't always see is what it takes to keep going after moments like that. You don't get time to sit with it. You don't get time to process it right away. You learn how to keep your focus, finish the assignment, and make sure nothing slips, because somebody is depending on you to do your job right. That kind of training stays with you. It teaches you how to separate what you feel from what you have to do. Not because the feelings aren't real, but because the responsibility in front of you is real too.

Over time, you develop a way of carrying it. You don't ignore it, but you don't let it control you either. You learn how to stay steady in situations that would shake most people. You learn how to think clearly when everything around you feels heavy. Even though you're trained to stay focused, you don't become numb. If anything, you become more aware. You start to recognize the quiet strength in people. The ones who don't say much, but show up anyway. The ones who are hurting, but still find a way to help someone else.

Those are the things that leave an impression. They shape how you see people. They shape how you move. You begin to understand that strength isn't about avoiding hard moments, it's about handling them and still doing what needs to be done. That's a different kind of mindset. One that doesn't come from comfort, but from experience. The older a person becomes, the more they begin to understand how quickly time moves. Years pass faster than we expect. Children grow up. Neighborhoods change. Friends and family members pass away. Sometimes you find yourself sitting quietly remembering moments from decades earlier as if they happened yesterday. I have reached a point in my life where memories have become a kind of living history.

Some of those memories bring laughter. Some bring sadness. But all of them remind me that life is a journey filled with lessons. If I could speak directly to younger generations, I would tell them this. Pay attention to the moments that are happening right now. Because one day those moments will become memories. And memories are one of the few things time cannot completely erase.

CHAPTER TWENTY-ONE
Mississippi Summers

Some of my strongest memories come from the trips we made to Mississippi. My mother was raised there, and whenever we visited it felt like stepping into a completely different world from the city streets of St. Louis. The pace of life in Mississippi moved slower. People talked longer. Meals lasted longer. Front porches became places where stories were shared late into the evening. For a young boy, those trips were exciting because there were always relatives everywhere. My mother had a large family, and every visit felt like a family reunion.

But those trips also came with lessons. Before we even arrived, my mother reminded us about how we were expected to behave. "Yes sir." "No sir." "Yes ma'am." "No ma'am." Respect was not optional. And we were warned not to make eye contact with white adults unless spoken to first. Those rules were difficult for a child to understand, but they were part of the reality of the South at that time. Looking back now, I realize my mother was doing what many parents did during those years. She was teaching us how to move safely through a world that did not always treat Black families fairly.

But Mississippi also gave us something valuable. It connected us to our roots. It allowed us to meet grandparents and great grandparents whose lives stretched back into a time much closer to slavery than most people today realize.

Those elders carried history in their voices. Stories about hard work. Stories about survival. Stories about faith. I wish now that I had asked more questions. But that is something many people realize later in life. You do not always understand the value of wisdom until the people who carried it are gone.

Every young man eventually reaches a point where childhood begins to fade and adulthood slowly takes its place. For me that transition happened gradually. Sports played a big role during those years. Basketball and softball gave me confidence and discipline. Being part of a team teaches you that success rarely happens alone. You rely on others. They rely on you. Winning the city championship in softball was one of those moments that made me feel proud of what we had accomplished together. But sports were only part of the story.

Watching the men in my family also shaped my understanding of what manhood meant. My father showed me the value of steady work. My uncle Charlie, the boxer, showed me the importance of strength and determination. Seeing him spar with Sonny Liston made an impression on me. When you witness someone from your own family standing in the same ring with a famous fighter, it changes the way you think about possibility. It makes you realize that greatness is not always something distant. Sometimes it is closer than you think.

Not everyone knows exactly what they want to do with their life. But for me, the idea of public service felt natural. Serving as a police officer and firefighter allowed me to do something meaningful for the community that had helped raise me. When you wear a uniform, you represent something larger than yourself. You represent safety. You represent trust. People expect you to act with professionalism and integrity. That responsibility can be heavy at times. But it is also honorable. I believed then, and I still believe now, that serving your community is one of the most important contributions a person can make. You may not become famous. You may never appear in newspapers. But the people whose lives you touch will remember. And sometimes that is enough.

Chapter Twenty-Two
The Hard Calls

Emergency work exposes you to moments that many people never see. Some calls involve small problems that can be solved quickly. Others involve situations that stay with you for years. The bicycle accident on the steep hill was one of those moments. Watching firefighters raise a car to reach a young man underneath it is something you do not forget. The fire where the child was found behind the stove is another memory that remains clear in my mind.

People often thank firefighters for their bravery. But the truth is that some calls leave a quiet weight in your heart. You replay the moment in your mind. You wonder if arriving a few minutes earlier might have changed the outcome. That is something many emergency responders carry with them. But we continue doing the work because the next call might be the one where a life is saved. And those moments matter. At seventy-eight years old, I have had time to think about what life has taught me. Some lessons were learned easily. Others came through hardship. But each one added something to my understanding of the world. I learned that courage is not the absence of fear. It is the decision to move forward despite it. I learned that people are capable of both kindness and cruelty.

Sometimes you will see both sides in the same person. I learned that life can change in seconds. One phone call. One accident. One unexpected moment. And everything looks different. But I also learned that resilience is part of the human spirit. People have an incredible ability to recover, rebuild, and continue moving forward. That strength is something I witnessed many times throughout my career. As people grow older, they begin thinking more about the idea of legacy. Legacy is not just about money or achievements. It is about the example you leave behind. Did you help people when they needed help? Did you treat others with fairness and respect? Did you live with integrity? Those questions matter more than titles or awards. When people remember you, they remember how you treated them. They remember the moments when you stood beside them during difficult times. That is the kind of legacy I hope my life reflects. Not perfection. But purpose.

CHAPTER TWENTY-THREE

Engine Company 27

When I graduated from the fire academy, I was assigned to Engine Company 27. At the time there were only two Black firefighters on my shift. Julius and me. Coming into the firehouse, I knew things might not be easy. The fire department, like many places during those years, was still adjusting to change. Some men welcomed it. Others did not. My captain made it clear early on that he did not want me there. He had his opinions, and they were not subtle. But the rest of the men on the shift treated me fairly. And when you are in a job where lives are on the line, that matters more than anything else. Fire does not care what color you are. When the alarm sounds, everyone has the same responsibility.

You either do the job, or you don't. During that same time in my life, something much more important happened. In October of 1973, my oldest daughter Tammy was born. Her mother's name was Cathy. Becoming a father changes a man. Suddenly the world is not just about you anymore. Everything you do begins to carry more weight, because someone else is depending on you. Around that time, I also joined the

Black Firefighters Association, one of the oldest organizations of Black firefighters. Groups like that existed because many of us understood that we had to support each other. Progress does not always happen automatically. Sometimes people have to push the door open.

Chapter Twenty-Four

Half the City on Fire

One night in the early 1970s I saw something that made a lasting impression on me. I remember looking out over downtown St. Louis and seeing fires burning across large sections of the city. From about three o'clock in the afternoon until nearly eight that early the next morning, buildings across downtown were burning. It was almost twenty-hours being up. At the time the city had many abandoned buildings, and fires could spread quickly through areas that had been neglected. Watching that scene, I remember thinking to myself, "Boy, I hope it's not like this all the time." Firefighting can be unpredictable. Some days are quiet. Other days feel like the entire city is calling for help at the same time. But those moments teach you something important. A firefighter's job is never routine. Every call is different. Every situation carries its own risks.

For a period of time I was doing something that most people would probably find exhausting. I was working for the police department and the fire department at the same time. There were days when I would leave the police department, take off one uniform, and go straight to the firehouse to put on another.

Trading one uniform for another. Looking back now, I wonder how I managed it. But when you are young and motivated, you find the energy. I believed in public service, and both jobs gave me the opportunity to help people. During my years in the police department, I made a personal decision about how I would do the job. I never wrote a ticket that wasn't deserved. Not one. But I did see other officers take advantage of people sometimes. Too often those people were poor, and too often they were Black.

Working inside the system gave me a chance to see how things really operated. Sometimes justice worked the way it should. But sometimes decisions were influenced by friendships and connections. I even spent time inside judges' chambers before court proceedings began, and I saw how conversations behind closed doors could shape outcomes. Some decisions were made on the golf course before anyone ever stepped into a courtroom. I tried to tell people what I was seeing, but many of them did not want to hear it. They believed the system was always fair. But life had already taught me that fairness is not automatic. Sometimes it requires people willing to speak the truth.

One day while working patrol as a police officer, I pulled over a car for speeding along Lucas and Hunt Road. It looked like an ordinary traffic stop at first, something that happens many times during a shift. But when I walked up to the driver's window, I realized the man behind the wheel was Dennis Edwards from the famous singing group The Temptations. Life has a funny way of putting unexpected moments in your path. Growing up, music from groups like The Temptations was part of the soundtrack of our lives. Their songs played on radios across the country, and people everywhere knew their voices. So, there I was, standing on the side of the road, realizing I had just stopped one of the most recognizable voices in music. We talked for a moment, and the situation stayed friendly. In the end, I let him go with a warning. Moments like that remind you that even famous people are just people living their lives like everyone else. Sometimes they make the same mistakes as the rest of us. But that traffic stop became one of those stories you remember years later because of how unexpected it was.

Growing up and working in many different environments, I often found myself in rooms where I was the only Black person present. That situation can be uncomfortable for some people, but it also teaches you something interesting about human nature. Sometimes people forget you are there. When they do, you hear conversations that they might not say if they were paying attention to who was in the room. Over the years I heard many things that helped me understand how some people truly felt about race in America.

Not everything I heard was positive. But those experiences gave me insight into how people think and how systems sometimes operate. Understanding people is important, especially in jobs where lives are involved. When you answer emergency calls, you cannot pick and choose who deserves help. When someone needs assistance, you respond. That was always my mindset. No matter who called, the job was to answer.

Chapter Twenty - Five
Family Was Everything

In 1985 I was promoted to Captain in the fire department. That promotion represented many years of experience, hard work, and dedication to the job. I was assigned to Engine Company 33. At that time, I was the only Black firefighter across all three shifts in that house, and the neighborhood surrounding the fire station was mostly white. I was thirty-eight years old. Looking back now, I sometimes wondered if the assignment was meant to test me. Some people may have believed the situation would cause problems or make leadership difficult. But the firefighters working there were experienced men. Many of them had been on the job longer than I had.

Leadership in the fire department is not about authority. It is about respect. And respect is earned through knowledge of the job, consistency, and the ability to make decisions when things become dangerous. Over time the men in that firehouse saw that I was committed to doing the job right. Once that became clear, the work moved forward just like it should. By the early 1990s I had spent many years serving in the fire department. I had worked different assignments, gained experience, and taken on leadership responsibilities. Like many firefighters who reach the rank of Captain, I decided to take the next step and sit for the Chief's exam. That exam required serious preparation. It tested knowledge of fire operations, leadership ability, department policies, and decision making.

When the results were announced, thirteen Black firefighters had passed the exam. For many of us, that moment felt like progress. It showed that years of work and experience were being recognized. But soon after the results came out, the department claimed that cheating had occurred. Because of that accusation, the entire test was thrown out. Just like that, the opportunity disappeared. For those of us who had studied and passed honestly, the decision was frustrating. It felt like a step backward after years of effort. But life teaches you that not every door opens when you expect it to. Sometimes you simply keep moving forward and focus on the work you were already doing. That is what I did.

Not every experience in my life came from public service. Sometimes life offered opportunities that had nothing to do with police work or firefighting. In 1978 I appeared on the television game show The Price Is Right. Standing on that stage was an unusual experience for someone who had spent most of his time responding to emergency calls. It was a moment that reminded me how unpredictable life can be. A couple of years later, in 1980, I had a small role in a movie called Delirium. The role fit my background perfectly. I played a police officer. It was not a large part, but it was interesting to see how film production worked behind the scenes. But the biggest surprise of my life came in August of 1981.

That was the day three daughters entered my life at the same time. Aimee. Ailisha. And Aileen. Triplets. Their mother's name was Dianne Reeves. When the doctors told me there would be three babies instead of one, I realized immediately that life was about to change in a major way. Watching my daughters grow, develop their personalities, and find their own paths became one of the most meaningful parts of my life. Every parent hopes their children grow into strong individuals. I was proud of all my daughters and the women they would eventually become.

WHAT I MEANT

I realized that I should have had fun while
I was a kid
because I know
that I'm not going to be ten again.
As soon as I become an adult.
I know
that I'm not going to be a baby again
like I wish I were.

I mean...
when you have a problem. like...
when you mess up on something,
you are going to look back and say.
'I wish I was that little girl again.
when I could have been,
instead of trying to grow up so fast.'

This is the end.
There isn't anymore
until...
I see that little girl I used to be.

Aimee Vaughn
Age: 11

Aimee Vaughn

CHAPTER TWENTY-SIX

Hurricane Gilbert

In 1989 I took on another unexpected role in life. I became the manager for Dennis Roberts, the flyweight kickboxing champion of the world. In the boxing world I used the name Hurricane Gilbert. Managing a world champion fighter brought me into an entirely different environment from firefighting and police work. Boxing events required planning, promotion, and organization. I was involved in helping arrange events and making sure everything ran smoothly. Dennis Roberts was an excellent fighter, and I was proud to be part of his success. We even made history by becoming the first Black boxing promotion in the state of Missouri. I still have pictures of myself standing in the ring holding his championship belt.

My oldest daughter Tami was a teenager at the time, and she helped out at some of the events. She worked the concession area selling popcorn during the fights. Those were good memories. Life sometimes gives you opportunities to step into worlds you never expected to see. Managing a world champion fighter was definitely one of those moments. I also knew Leon and Michael Spinks when they were still amateur boxers, just putting in the work and trying to make a name for themselves. At the time, they were focused, disciplined, and serious about what they were doing. You could see it in how they trained and carried themselves. Would you believe they both went on to become heavyweight champions of the world.

That's something that stays with you. Watching people in the early stages, before the recognition, before the titles, and then seeing where they end up. It reminds you that what looks small in the moment can turn into something major over time. My own path crossed with that world in a different way. I had the opportunity to walk many fighters to the ring at

Mandalay Bay, being part of those moments when everything is on the line. The energy, the focus, the silence right before the crowd erupts, it's something you don't forget.

I've even walked UFC fighters to the Octagon. Different sport, same intensity. Same level of preparation and mental focus. You see firsthand what it takes to step into that kind of environment. Being around that taught me something. Success doesn't just happen in the spotlight. It's built long before anyone is watching. It's built in the early mornings, the repetition, the discipline, and the mindset to keep going when nobody is paying attention. Seeing it up close gave me a deeper respect for the process, not just the outcome.

By the early 2000s I had spent many years wearing two uniforms during my life. First as a police officer and then as a firefighter. Those careers allowed me to serve my community and experience things most people never see. In 1993 I retired from the police department after twenty years of service. Twenty years is a long time to spend answering calls, responding to emergencies, and witnessing the many sides of human nature. During that time, I saw courage, fear, tragedy, and kindness. Some days were quiet. Other days were filled with situations that stayed with me long after the shift ended. But through it all, I tried to do the job with fairness and integrity. After many years of service in the fire department, that chapter of my life eventually came to a close as well. I retired in 2001. For the first time in many years, I no longer had to wait for alarms or late-night calls. Retirement can feel strange for people who have spent their lives working in demanding professions. You go from constant movement to suddenly having time to slow down. But life was not finished offering new experiences.

In 2002, I met the love of my life, Evangeline, who we call Vangel. By that time in my life, I had already experienced a lot. I had seen the world in many ways, but meeting her brought a different kind of peace. She has been by my side for over twenty years, and together we have built something strong. We have shared many beautiful memories and traveled the world together, seeing places I once only dreamed about as a young boy growing up in St. Louis. What I appreciate most is the companionship. Having someone who stands with you, understands you, and walks with you through life means more than anything to me. At this stage in my life, I understand that love, peace, and shared experiences are what truly matter.

Las Vegas is a very different place from the neighborhoods where I grew up. The city never really sleeps. Lights fill the night sky, and people from every corner of the world pass through the casinos and hotels every day. After retiring, I made the decision to move to Las Vegas. Years earlier I had built a house there in 1992 and rented it out while I was still living in St. Louis. Eventually the time came when it made sense to make the move myself.

Working at the Mandalay Bay gave me the opportunity to meet many well-known people from the worlds of sports, entertainment, and music. Over time I crossed paths with celebrities like Elizabeth Taylor, Sean Connery, Tiger Woods, Michael Jordan, Will Smith, Kevin Hart, Rihanna, Charles Barkley, Stevie Wonder, Alicia Keys, Bernard Hopkins, Joe Frazier, Derek Jeter, Floyd Mayweather, and Roy Jones Jr. Earth,

Wind & Fire also performed there. Each encounter reminded me of something important. Fame does not change the fact that everyone is still human. Behind the lights, cameras, and attention, people are simply living their lives just like everyone else. For me, the job was about making sure guests were safe and that everything operated smoothly. It was another form of service, just in a different setting.

Chapter Twenty- Seven

A Black Hero

When you reach a certain age, you start to spend more time reflecting on the road you traveled. My life began in 1947 in St. Louis, Missouri. I grew up on Thomas Street in a neighborhood where horses still pulled carts through the alleys and families burned trash in metal barrels. I remember ice men delivering blocks of ice before refrigerators became common. I remember waiting for a white horse that never arrived. I watched the country change during the Civil Rights era. I traveled across the world from Alaska to South Africa. I served my community as both a police officer and a firefighter. I had five beautiful children and built a life that included moments I never could have predicted. I stood in boxing rings managing a world champion fighter. I appeared on a television game show. I even had a small role in a movie. And later in life I found myself working in a Las Vegas casino meeting some of the most famous people in the world. Looking back, the road from Thomas Street to all those places seems almost unbelievable. But that is the way life works. You start in one place and never really know where the journey will lead.

After seventy-eight years of living, I have learned a few lessons worth sharing. First, life moves faster than you expect. One day you are a child watching your father build a walkway in front of your home. The next thing you know, decades have passed and you are the one telling the stories. Second, people matter more than things. Houses disappear. Neighborhoods change. But the people who shared those moments with you remain part of your life forever. Third, courage matters. My mother taught me that when she sent my brother and me back into the grocery store, we were afraid to enter. Fear will stop you if you let it. But courage pushes you forward. Fourth, life is unpredictable. Sometimes opportunities appear where you least expect them. The key is being ready when they arrive. And finally, remember not to take life too seriously. Nobody gets out alive anyway. So, enjoy the ride while you are here. Laugh when you can. Learn when you must. And try to leave the world a little better than you found it.

I first met Leon and Michael Spinks when they were young amateur boxers in St. Louis. Little did anyone know that those two brothers from the projects would one day become heavyweight champions of the world. Leon defeated Muhammad Ali, and Michael defeated Larry Holmes. That is an extraordinary accomplishment for any family. What I admired most about the Spinks brothers was their determination. They recognized their gifts, worked hard, and made the most of every opportunity. Their journey proves that success is not determined by where you come from, but by what you choose to do with the talents God has given you. Not everyone is meant to be a rocket scientist, but everyone has the ability to excel at something.

One last memory comes to mind. A fellow graduate from my police academy class, Larry Cockrell, later made history as the first African American Director of the United States Secret Service. He eventually led President Bill Clinton's security detail. After meeting Larry, I knew he was destined for greatness. There was something special about the way he carried himself. He treated people with kindness and respect, remained down-to-earth, and possessed remarkable intelligence. In many ways, he reminded me of President Barack Obama.

As I reflect on the people, experiences, triumphs, and challenges that shaped my life, I realize that ordinary people can accomplish extraordinary things. No matter where life begins, character, perseverance, faith, and hard work can take you farther than you ever imagined. My hope is that these stories have reminded you that your past does not define your future. Keep dreaming, keep striving, and never underestimate what is possible. The title of this book is A Black Hero. Some people may hear that title and imagine someone larger than life. A person who performed incredible acts that changed history. But the truth is that heroes are often ordinary people. A hero is someone who shows up when they are needed. Someone who chooses service over comfort. Someone who stands firm when things become difficult. Throughout my life I tried to do exactly that.

I answered calls when people needed help. I served my community as both a police officer and firefighter. I worked hard to build a life for my family. And I carried the lessons my parents taught me wherever I went. I was not famous. I was not wealthy. But I lived a life full of experiences, challenges, and opportunities. And if my story teaches anything, it is this: Ordinary people can live extraordinary lives. You do not have to be perfect. You just have to show up, do your best, and keep moving forward. If you can do that, you have already become something important. Maybe even a hero.

Before I bring these stories to a close and call it a night, I plan to sit back and listen to three of my favorite songs: Wake Up Everybody by Teddy Pendergrass, When You've Been Blessed by Patti LaBelle, and The Greatest Love of All by Whitney Houston. Those songs remind me to stay grateful, keep believing, and never stop growing.

Reflections From Friends

Hearing how others describe your impact provides a different perspective. It highlights moments that may not stand out from your own point of view but hold meaning for others. Those reflections add depth to the overall story. They show how actions taken over time influenced the people around you. They demonstrate that consistency and character leave a lasting impression. Each reflection represents a connection. It reflects how experiences were shared and how those moments were remembered. That perspective reinforces the idea that impact extends beyond individual experience. It continues through the people who carry those memories forward.

Dennis Roberts "Mongoose"
St. Louis World Champion Kickboxer

Dennis Roberts, known in the boxing world as "Mongoose," shared that he was the one who gave Gilbert Vaughn the nickname "Hurricane." According to Dennis, the name fit Gilbert perfectly because when a hurricane moves through, it changes everything in its path. Dennis explained that Gilbert had that same kind of impact on people's lives. His manger style, energy, determination, and belief in others helped open doors and create opportunities. Dennis credits Gilbert Vaughn for playing a major role in his career. He said that Gilbert's support and guidance helped shape his success and that his career would not have been what it became without him. Dennis expressed deep gratitude for Gilbert's influence and the role he played in helping him reach the level he achieved in the world of kickboxing.

Kevin Phillips
St. Louis Locomotive Engineer

I remember watching Mr. Vaughn go to work as both a firefighter and a police officer when I was a kid, and I was always amazed that he managed to do both. He was consistently kind and welcoming to the kids in the neighborhood, and we all admired the Lincoln Town Cars he drove. I also remember when his fire company responded to my parents' house for a gas leak. When he realized it was his neighbor's home, you could see how genuinely concerned he was for our safety. That moment stayed with me.

Adam Long Platoon Fire Chief
St. Louis Airport Fire Department

I had the opportunity to meet Gilbert Vaughn back in 1978 through my cousin, Reggie Long, who worked with him on the St. Louis Police Department. From the very beginning, I remember being impressed by the fact that he was serving as both a firefighter and a police officer at the same time. Back then, that was not something you heard of. I didn't know anyone else doing both, and it spoke volumes about his work ethic and commitment to service.

If there is one thing I can say about Gilbert, it's that he has always been a genuinely good man, both in and out of the fire department. What stood out to me the most was his presence. He carried himself with confidence, but also with kindness. And I will never forget his smile. It was big, real, and welcoming. The kind of smile that made people feel at ease and let you know exactly what kind of person he was.

Deputy Fire Chief Derrick Phillips
St. Louis Fire Department

In the history of the St. Louis Fire Department, there are certain names that carry real weight. For me, that name is Captain Gilbert Vaughn. He wasn't just a supervisor, he was one of the reasons I chose this profession and committed my life to the fire service.

Captain Vaughn was the heart of Engine Company 10. If you knew "The 10s," then you already understood the level of work and expectation that came with it. He led from the front and earned his respect on the fireground, not from a title, but from doing the work. He saw a tremendous amount of fire duty, and time after time, he showed what it meant to stay calm under pressure and make the right decisions when it mattered most. Watching him work was a lesson in itself. You didn't have to be told what leadership looked like, you could see it. Like many others, I always believed he should have been promoted to Battalion Chief. He had the leadership, the respect of the firefighters, and the experience that you can't teach. That decision will always be hard to understand.

But instead of letting that create frustration, it pushed me. Seeing someone like Captain Vaughn, who earned everything through his work, made me want to go further. It motivated me to continue my education and pursue advancement, making sure that the standard he set would continue. To this day, when we talk about leadership in the firehouse, his name still comes up. I still think about the kind of Chief he would have been, fair, strong, and committed to his people. His impact didn't stop at his rank. It lives on through those of us he influenced.

www.ingramcontent.com/pod-product-compliance
Lightning Source LLC
LaVergne TN
LVHW010612110826
845149LV00003B/882